W9-DGN-669

To Ava ~
love Nona ~ ♡

Goodnight St. Louis

June Herman

Julia Dubroy

Karen Heyse

GOODNIGHT ST. LOUIS

JUNE HERMAN & JULIE DUBRAY
ILLUSTRATED BY KAREN HEYSE

SAINT LOUIS

Copyright © 2013 by Skip to My Lou, LLC
www.goodnightstlouis.com
June Herman and Julie Dubray

First Edition – June 2013

ISBN
978-1-4602-1580-7 (Hardcover)

All rights reserved.

All rights reserved. No part of this book may be reproduced or transmitted in any form or by any means, electronic or mechanical, including photocopying, recording or by any information storage and retrieval system without written permission from the Publisher.

St. Louis Blues name and logo are trademarks of the NHL Team. © NHL 2013. All Rights Reserved. Used with permission.

Printed and Bound in Canada

Produced by:

FriesenPress
Suite 300 – 852 Fort Street
Victoria, BC, Canada V8W 1H8

www.friesenpress.com

Major League Baseball trademarks and copyrights are used with permission of Major League Baseball Properties, Inc.

With love to friends and family who
gave their unending support and
encouragement; especially our husbands,
Drew and Roger, and our children Taylor,
Cory, and Christian, Andrea and Michael.
And Max & Sawyer too!

Goodnight St. Louis with so much to share,

From the Arch to the Zoo
and balloons in the air.

Goodnight to the Arch, "Gateway to the West."
The view from the top is always the best!

Goodnight Laclede's Landing and streets made of brick. Goodnight carriage rides and horses so quick.

Goodnight
Old Courthouse,
lit up at night.
Goodnight
to our flags
waving red,
blue,
and white.

Goodnight city parks and turtles that play.
Goodnight Citygarden and fountains that spray.

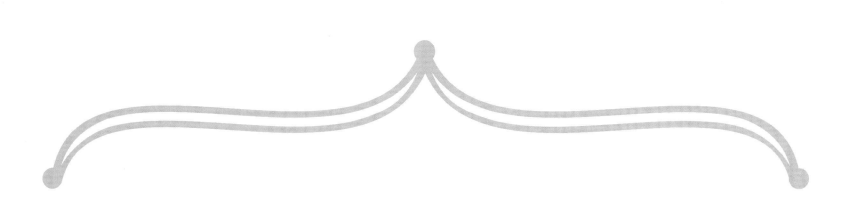

Goodnight to cathedrals, one Old and one New.

Goodnight historic mansions in colorful hues.

Goodnight
Union Station,
once a busy depot.

Goodnight beautiful
fountain in the Plaza Aloe.

Goodnight Art Museum
with objects so rare.

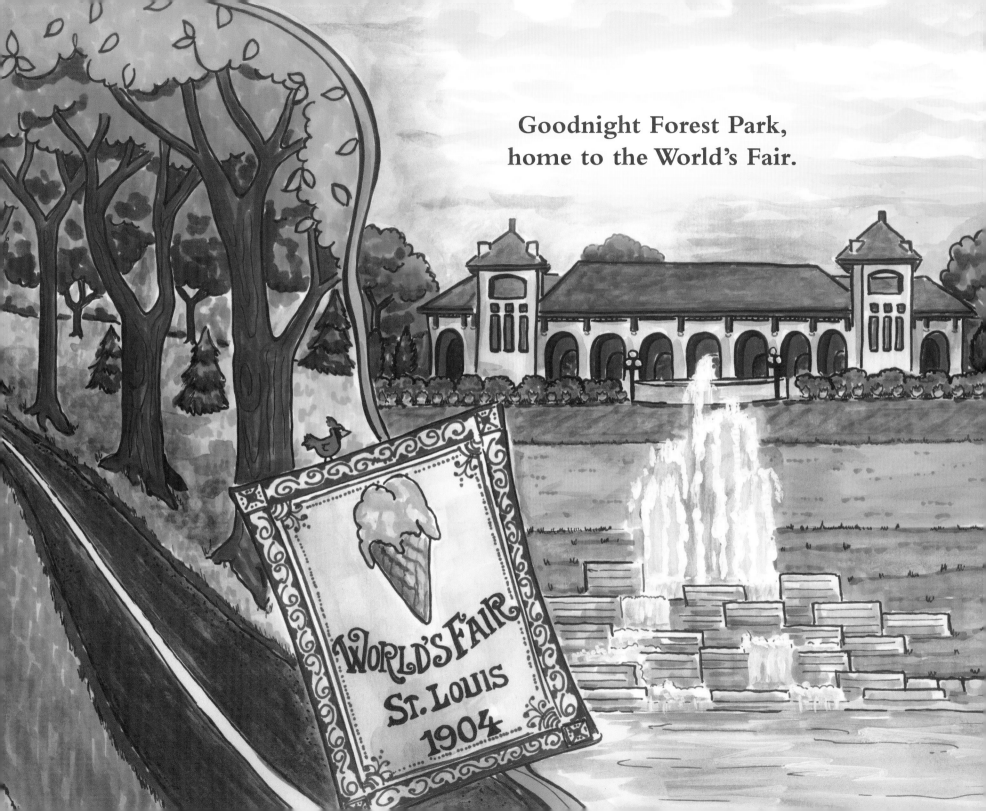

Goodnight Forest Park,
home to the World's Fair.

WORLD'S FAIR
ST. LOUIS
1904

Goodnight Butterfly House where beauty takes flight.
Goodnight to the Garden's concerts in the moonlight.

Goodnight
History Museum,
where our past
comes alive.

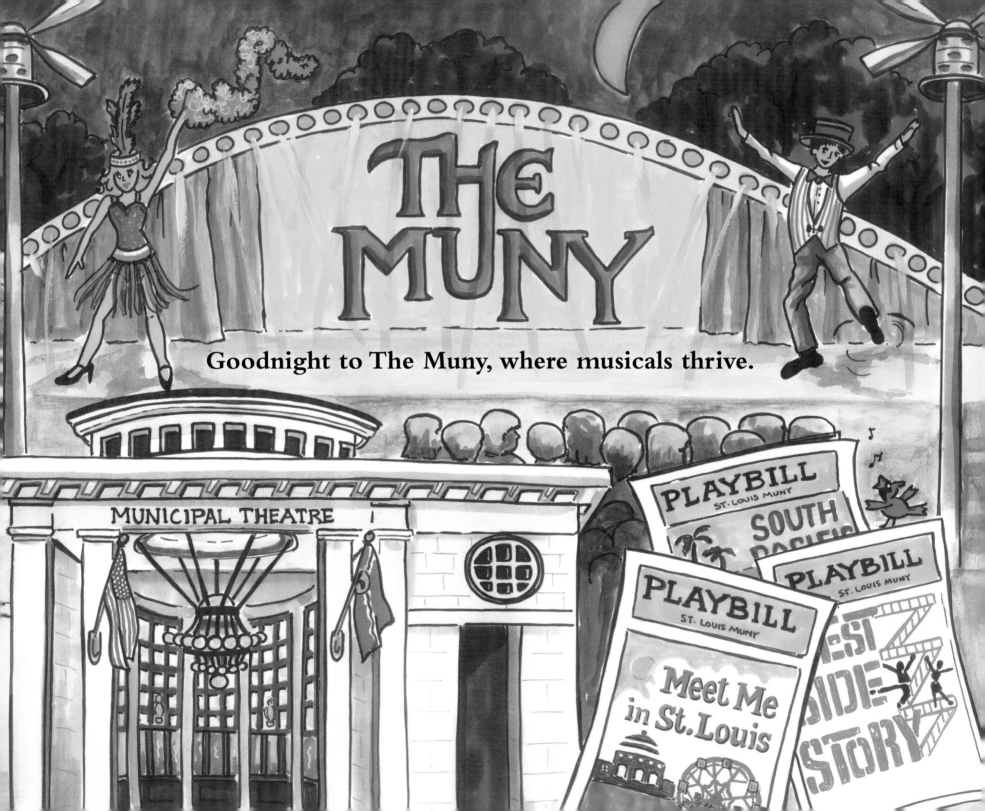

Goodnight to The Muny, where musicals thrive.

Goodnight to Ted Drewes frozen concretes.
Goodnight to Crown Candy's mouth-watering eats.

Goodnight City Museum's rooftop bus
and slippery slides.

Goodnight Magic House and
hair-raising good times.

Goodnight Grant's Farm's Clydesdales and cows that say "MOO!"

Goodnight to all creatures in the Saint Louis Zoo.

Goodnight colorful fairs and lively parades,

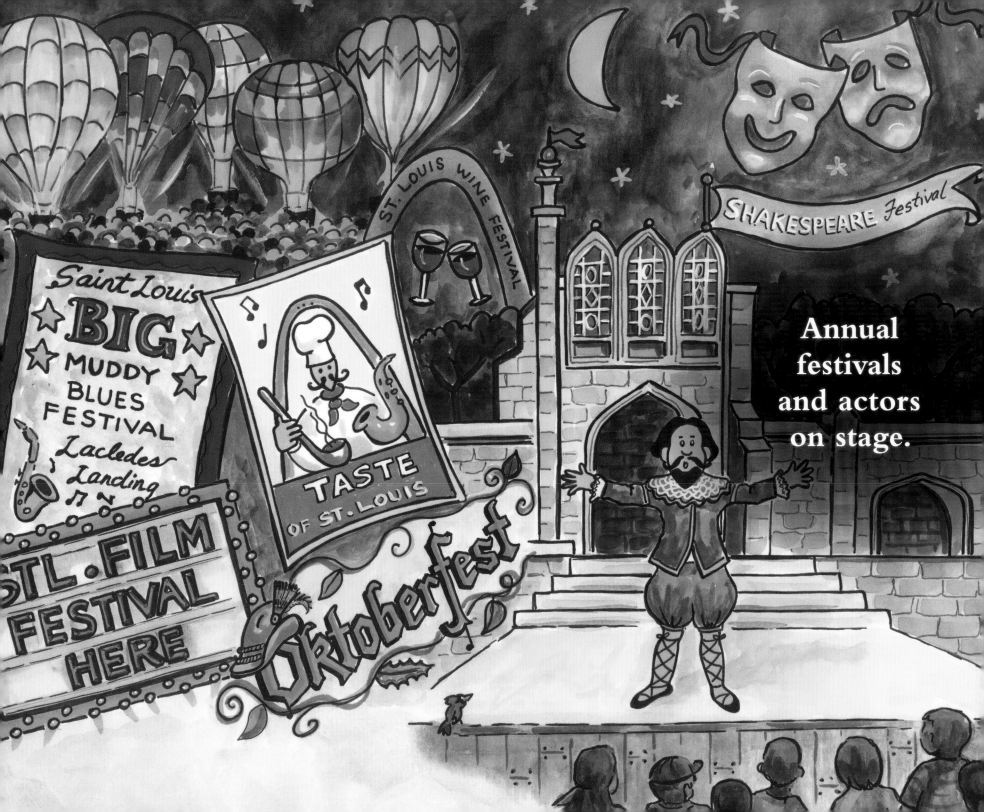

Goodnight Science Center and roaring dinosaurs.

Goodnight Planetarium, where space is explored.

Goodnight to our home teams: Rams, Cardinals, and Blues.
No matter the season, we always stay true!

Goodnight Powell Hall and Fabulous Fox.
Goodnight to musicians playing jazz, blues, and rock.

Goodnight to St. Louis,
  we bid you adieu.

Our beloved Gateway City,
there's no place like you!

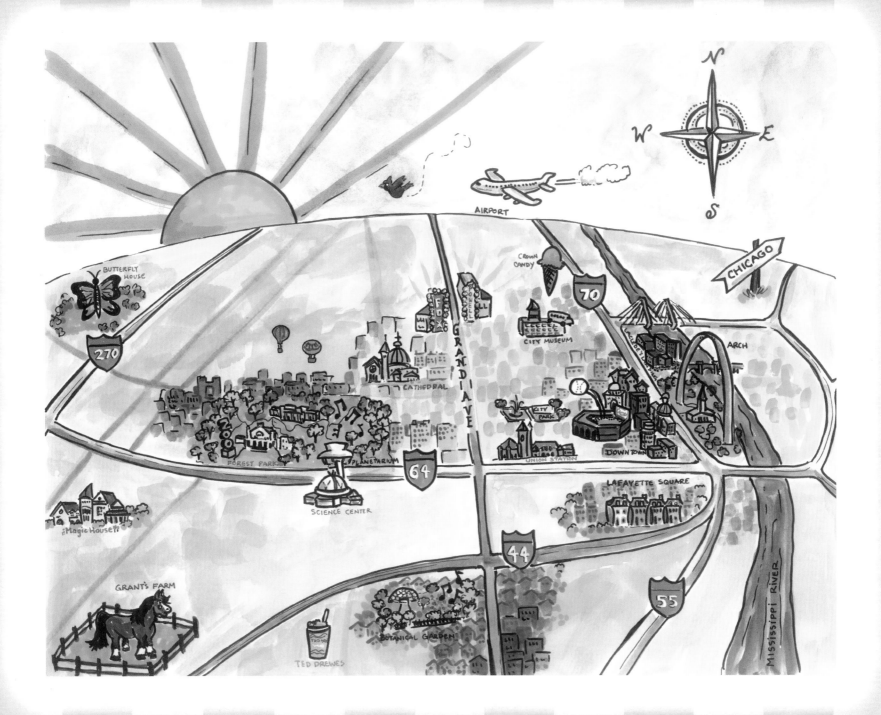

St. Louis, MO

Founded in 1764 by Pierre Laclede and Auguste Chouteau and named for King Louis IX of France, the city of St. Louis has a rich history and a vibrant culture. Often referred to as "The Gateway City," St. Louis was the starting point for many explorers and travelers heading west, including Lewis and Clark. Following the Louisiana Purchase and because of its location on the Mississippi River, St. Louis became a major port city. Traders, trappers, and merchants used the river to transport goods downriver to New Orleans and upstream to eastern cities. Today you can still see steamboats as well as river barges filled with goods and materials as they make their way from St. Louis to markets around the world.

The Gateway Arch

The most recognized landmark in St. Louis, the Gateway Arch is located in the National Park Service's Jefferson National Expansion Memorial. Built as a monument to the westward expansion of the United States, the Arch is the tallest man-made monument in the country. The "Gateway to the West" stands an impressive 630-feet tall and is 630-feet wide at its base. Visitors can get a bird's eye view of the city and the Mississippi riverfront by riding a tram all the way to the top. Below the Arch, the Museum of Westward Expansion provides a unique glimpse into the lives of the explorers, pioneers, and native peoples who helped shape the American West. Designed by architect Eero Saarinen, the Arch was completed in 1965 after 2 ½ years of construction. It opened to the public in 1967.

Laclede's Landing

Laclede's Landing, or The Landing, is a nine-block area in downtown St. Louis on the banks of the Mississippi River, just north of the Eads Bridge. The Landing's cobblestone streets and century-old brick buildings keep our city's past alive in this bustling entertainment district. Visitors can enjoy horse-drawn carriage rides along the riverfront below the Arch grounds or stroll along the 100-year-old bridge. Built in 1874, Eads Bridge is a combined foot, railway, and road bridge and was once the longest arch bridge in the world.

The Old Courthouse

Once the tallest building in the state of Missouri and more than 150 years old, the Old Courthouse is part of the Jefferson National Expansion Memorial. Many famous cases were tried here. In 1846, slave Dred Scott sued the United States in order to win freedom for himself and his wife, Harriet. Open for daily visits, the Old Courthouse is also listed in the National Park Service's National Underground Railroad Network to Freedom.

The Missouri State Flag

Missouri became a state in August 1821, but did not have a state flag until 1913. Similarly colored to the American flag, the Missouri flag has three large stripes of color: red, white, and blue. The red stripe stands for valor, the white stripe stands for purity, and the blue stripe stands for justice. The state seal in the flag's center shows that Missouri is an independent state within the United States, and that it is located in the center of the country. There are 24 stars around the seal to show that Missouri was the 24th state admitted to the Union.

The Flag of the City of St. Louis

The City of St. Louis flag was designed by Yale University professor, Theodore Sizer. The wavy blue lines on the flag represent the two major rivers that come together and flow through St. Louis, the Mississippi and the Missouri. The blue fleur-de-lis on the gold circle illustrates our city's French heritage.

St. Louis City Parks

St. Louis is home to 111 city parks covering more than 3,000 acres in over 40 neighborhoods. Families love to picnic, play ball, walk dogs, or just stroll along the miles of trails and pathways. Many parks have ornamental lakes, boathouses, playgrounds, and athletic fields. Others boast formal gardens, monuments, and statues. No matter what you enjoy, you're sure to relax in one of St. Louis's beautiful parks.

Turtle Park

Opened in 1996, Turtle Park is a unique and award-winning playground on the south side of Forest Park, near the Saint Louis Zoo. Visitors delight in the seven concrete turtles and two concrete snakes that invite kids of all ages to climb and play on their backs and picnic beside them in the cool green grass.

Citygarden

An urban oasis, Citygarden is unlike any other downtown park. Opened in July 2009, Citygarden was designed to be part sculpture garden and part water park, with lush plantings, stonework, and architectural features. Citygarden's landscape takes its cues from the St. Louis region's most notable feature, its great rivers. Two dozen works of modern and contemporary sculpture by world-class artists keep company with a six-foot waterfall and a spray plaza. 102 nozzles shoot water as high as six feet into the air in thousands of patterns and colors. Open every day, with no admission charged, Citygarden is within walking distance of the Arch, The Landing and other downtown attractions.

The Basilica of Saint Louis, King of France

The Basilica of Saint Louis, King of France is commonly known as the Old Cathedral. Located in downtown St. Louis adjacent to the Arch grounds, the Old Cathedral was completed in 1834 and was the first cathedral west of the Mississippi. Built on land set aside by city founders Pierre Laclede and Auguste Chouteau, the cathedral was named for our city's namesake, King Louis IX of France.

The Cathedral Basilica of Saint Louis

The Cathedral Basilica of Saint Louis is also known as the New Cathedral. Construction began in 1907 and was completed in 1914 when the first Mass was held. The New Cathedral is best known for its beautiful mosaics. Among the largest collection in the world, the cathedral's mosaic installation covers 83,000 square feet and includes more than 7,000 colors. Artists worked more than 75 years to complete the dazzling interior.

Historic Mansions and Neighborhoods

St. Louis is a city of neighborhoods. The colorful mansions in our illustration represent the "painted ladies," a colorful collection of Victorian-era homes located in Lafayette Square. St. Louis neighborhoods are vibrant communities with an interesting and eclectic blend of architectural styles, residents, and amenities.

St. Louis Union Station

Opened in 1894, St. Louis Union Station was once the largest and busiest passenger railroad terminal in the world. The original station included three main areas: the Headhouse, the Midway, and the Train Shed. The Headhouse included a hotel, restaurant, passenger waiting rooms, and ticket offices. Still in use today by a luxury hotel, the Headhouse area features a gold-leaf Grand Hall with a 65-foot barrel-vaulted ceiling and stained glass windows. At its busiest, the Train Shed housed more than 20 different railroads and, at the time, boasted the largest roof span in the world. In 1903, the station was expanded to welcome visitors to the 1904 World's Fair.

Aloe Plaza and "The Meeting of the Waters" Fountain

Directly across from Union Station is Aloe Plaza. Named for Louis P. Aloe, President of the St. Louis Board of Alderman from 1916-1923, the plaza is home to "The Meeting of the Waters" fountain. Designed by Carl Milles and completed in 1939, the fountain is a St. Louis favorite. Mythical male and female figures representing the Mississippi and Missouri rivers, as well as their many tributaries, celebrate the coming together of the waters that become the Mighty Mississippi.

Saint Louis Art Museum

Perched atop Art Hill with Saint Louis himself on guard, the Saint Louis Art Museum is "Dedicated to Art and Free to All." Originally built as part of the Palace of Fine Arts for the 1904 World's Fair, the Main Building was the sole structure from the Fair designed to be permanent. The newest addition to the Museum, the East Building, was completed in 2013. The Saint Louis Art Museum houses more than 33,000 works of art and includes pieces from nearly every culture and time period.

Forest Park

Opened in 1876, Forest Park has been called the heart and soul of St. Louis. The 1300-acre urban park has hosted events large and small over its 130-year history, including the 1904 World's Fair and the Summer Olympics. The park is home to many cultural attractions, scenic bike and foot paths, four 9-hole golf courses, tennis courts, a skating rink, a boathouse, and several restaurants. The Great Forest Park Balloon Race is held annually in Forest Park as are many other arts, music, and heritage festivals.

Missouri History Museum

Dedicated in 1913, the Missouri History Museum building was constructed with proceeds from the 1904 World's Fair to honor President Thomas Jefferson's role in the Louisiana Purchase. Built on the site of the main entrance to the Fair, the History Museum is home to a vast collection of art, artifacts, historical documents, and photographs chronicling Missouri history.

The Muny

The Municipal Theatre Association of St. Louis, or The Muny for short, is the oldest and largest outdoor musical theater in America. The first production, Robin Hood, was held in June 1919, and musicals continue to be performed every summer from mid-June through mid-August. The theater seats 11,000 with 1,500 free seats available for every production on a first-come, first-served basis.

City Museum

Housed in a former shoe warehouse, the 600,000-square-foot City Museum, located in downtown St. Louis, is a mixture of children's playground, funhouse, surrealistic pavilion, and architectural marvel. Every object in the museum is recycled, or found art, from the city itself—including old smokestacks, salvaged bridges, an old bus (parked overhanging the roof), a seven-story slide, miles of tile, and even abandoned airplanes. Opened in 1997 by creator Bob Cassilly, City Museum is a hands-on sensory thrill ride for the young and old.

The Magic House®

The St. Louis region's first interactive children's museum, The Magic House provides children of all ages and abilities the opportunity to experiment, create, and develop problem-solving skills. Kids can touch an electrically-charged ball, service a car, ring a replica Liberty Bell, and produce a musical bubble — all before lunch. Housed in a turn-of-the century Victorian mansion in suburban St. Louis, The Magic House has welcomed more than 10 million visitors since it opened in October 1979.

Sophia M. Sachs Butterfly House

Home to more than 1,000 free-flying butterflies from around the world and closer to home, the Butterfly House includes an 8,000-square-foot indoor conservatory where guests can get up close and personal with their winged friends. Located in suburban St. Louis, the Butterfly House opened in September 1998 and became part of the Missouri Botanical Garden in July 2001.

Missouri Botanical Garden

Founded by Henry Shaw and opened in 1859, the 79-acre Missouri Botanical Garden is beloved by St. Louisans and visitors alike. One of the oldest botanical gardens in the United States, and among the top three in the world, the Garden welcomes thousands of visitors every year to its annual displays, outdoor concerts, heritage festivals, and education and conservation events. Among its many attractions are the world-famous Climatron, the first geodesic dome to be used as a conservatory; Seiwa-en, a traditionally authentic Japanese garden; and the Doris I. Schnuck Children's Garden: A Missouri Adventure. The Garden is located in the historic Shaw neighborhood.

Ted Drewes Frozen Custard

A local tennis champion, Ted Drewes Sr. opened his first frozen custard stand with a traveling carnival in Florida in 1929. Fueled by his initial success, Ted opened stands in St. Louis, the first in 1930 on Natural Bridge Road, and the second the following year on South Grand Avenue. In 1941, he opened a third stand on historic Route 66 (Chippewa Street). Ted Drewes Frozen Custard has made the iconic "concrete," a shake or malt so thick you can turn it upside down, popular across the nation. Get in line for a Cardinal Sin, Fox Treat, or Terramizzou. As Ted Jr. says…"It really IS good guys…and gals!"

Crown Candy Kitchen

The long lines on the near north side are for Crown Candy Kitchen, a St. Louis tradition since 1913. Opened by Greek confectioners Harry Karandzieff and his best friend, Pete Jugaloff, a visit to Crown Candy is like stepping back in time. Wooden booths, soda fountains, and vintage jukeboxes on each table all lead visitors to believe that time has stood still. Known for delicious sandwiches, chili, hotdogs, ice cream, and handmade chocolates, nobody leaves Crown Candy without dessert; it's family policy. Take the "5 Malt Challenge"… if you dare!

Grant's Farm

Ancestral home of the Busch Family, Grant's Farm is a 281-acre attraction located southwest of St. Louis. More than 900 animals representing 100 species from six of the seven continents call Grant's Farm home, including the world-famous Budweiser Clydesdales. Eighteenth President Ulysses S. Grant, once farmed a portion of the land, and his four-room, two-story log cabin can still be seen on the property. A St. Louis tradition for over 50 years, 24 million guests have visited Grant's Farm, always free of charge.

Saint Louis Zoological Park

More than 19,000 animals call the Saint Louis Zoo home. Among the best zoos in the country, it is a recognized leader in animal research, management, conservation, and education. Plus, it's just plain fun! Millions of visitors have enjoyed rides on the 1½ mile Zooline Railroad and on the Mary Ann Lee Conservation Carousel, caught the Sea Lion Show, and visited Penguin and Puffin Coast. In fact, there are nearly 20 different animal houses, exhibits, and attractions to see at the 100-year-old Zoo. Open 363 days a year, there is never an attendance charge to visit.

Fairs, Festivals, and Parades

There is always something happening in St. Louis: Mardi Gras, St. Patrick's Day, Fair St. Louis, the Shakespeare Festival. St. Louis is a city that loves to celebrate its rich cultural heritage and its deep-rooted traditions.

Saint Louis Science Center and James S. McDonnell Planetarium

Originally founded in 1963, the Science Center has more than 700 hands-on exhibits in a three-building complex of over 300,000 square feet. It is among the largest science museums in the country and one of the top five science centers in the United States. Visitors can encounter a life-sized animated T rex, enjoy innovative "Amazing Science" demonstrations, and clock the speed of highway traffic below them from the pedestrian bridge that stretches over highway 64/40. The Planetarium features the Boeing Space Station and the Orthwein StarBay, where 9,000 stars are projected onto an 80-foot dome. The Science Center also features the high-fidelity OMNIMAX® Theater where viewers can become fully immersed in awe-inspiring scenery via a four-story screen in a wrap-around, state-of-the-art domed theater.

Our Home Teams

Called "The Best Sports City in America," St. Louis has something to cheer about. The St. Louis Cardinals, among the oldest franchises in Major League Baseball, have been World Series champs 11 times (and counting), making their home at Busch Stadium. The St. Louis Blues take to the ice each winter at the Scottrade Center, while our St. Louis Rams do battle on the Edward Jones Dome's gridiron.

Powell Symphony Hall

Originally built in 1925 as the St. Louis Theatre, Powell Hall became the permanent home of the world-class St. Louis Symphony Orchestra in 1968. Among the world's finest concert halls, Powell Hall was modeled after the royal chapel at Versailles (France) and includes a stained-glass window featuring an image of Saint Louis IX, King of France, on horseback. The St. Louis Symphony is the second oldest orchestra in the United States. The concert season begins in September and runs through the end of June.

The Fabulous Fox Theatre

The Fox Theatre, also known as "The Fabulous Fox," began as a movie palace in 1929. Today, the Fox offers a wide variety of entertainment including Broadway productions, concerts, and dance performances. The interior of the Fox is nothing short of opulent, with its jeweled and gilded elephants, lions, monkeys, peacocks, and swans; rajahs armed with swords; and a 5,280-pound, 12-foot jeweled-glass chandelier. No time to see a show? Tour the Fox on Tuesday, Thursday, and Saturday mornings (except holidays) for a nominal fee.

For additional copies and to learn more about the attractions and landmarks noted in Goodnight St. Louis, please visit our website
www.goodnightstlouis.com

Acknowledgements

Special thanks to the following for their assistance
in the research of this book:

Anheuser-Busch/Grant's Farm

Basilica of Saint Louis, King of France

Cathedral Basilica of Saint Louis

Citygarden

City Museum

Crown Candy Kitchen

Fabulous Fox Theatre

Laclede's Landing

Missouri Botanical Garden

Missouri History Museum

Saint Louis Art Museum

Saint Louis Science Center

Saint Louis Zoo

St. Louis Blues/National Hockey League

St. Louis Cardinals/Major League Baseball

St. Louis Convention & Visitors Commission

St. Louis Department of Parks, Recreation, and Forestry

St. Louis Rams

St. Louis Symphony

St. Louis Union Station

Ted Drewes Frozen Custard

The Gateway Arch

The Magic House

The Muny